An artist's perspective of posthumanism and AI

An artist's perspective of posthumanism and AI

Euan Rutter

An imprint of Boom Publications Ltd

272 Bath Street
Glasgow SCOTLAND
G2 4JR

Boom Graduates and the logo are trademarks of Boom Publications Ltd.

Boom Publications Ltd is a more-than-profit company, dedicating over half our profits to university scholarships for underprivileged students worldwide. In order to offset our carbon footprint, we also pledge to plant a tree for each graduation book commissioned.

An artist's perspective of posthumanism and AI
was first published in Great Britain in 2022.

Copyright © Euan Rutter. Euan Rutter has asserted his right under the
Copyright, Designs and Patents Act, 1988,
to be identified as Author of this work.
For legal purposes any Acknowledgements constitute
an extension of this copyright page.
Cover design by Boom Graduates Ltd and the Book Cover Zone USA.

All rights are reserved. No part of this publication may be reproduced or transmitted in any form or by any means, electronic or mechanical, including photocopying, recording, or any information storage or retrieval system, without prior permission in writing from the publishers.

Boom Publications Ltd do not have any control over, or responsibility for any third-party websites referred to or in this book. All internet addresses given in this book were correct at the time of going to press. The author and publisher regret any inconvenience if addresses have changed or sites have ceased to exist, but can accept no responsibility for any such changes.

Typeset by Helen at Boom Graduates.
Printed and bound in the UK.

To find out more about our authors and books visit www.boomgraduates.com
and sign up for our newsletters.

An artist's perspective of posthumanism and AI

Euan Rutter

Contents

Author biography...7
Abstract 9
Introduction 11
Chapter one 17
   Back to the Future 17
Chapter 2 29
   Looking Into the Beyond 29
Chapter 3 35
   Into the Matrix..35
Chapter 4 41
   Without Purpose 41
Chapter 5 45
   Where Art Thou?..45
Conclusion 53

References 59
A note about Boom Graduates 65
BOOM! 69
Notes 71

Author biography

The once-prolific art student, Euan Rutter, is a recent graduate from the Duncan of Jordanstone College of Art and Design (DJCAD), University of Dundee, recently voted the number one art school in Scotland... if not the WORLD! Euan holds a First Class BA (Hons) in Fine Art. During his time at DJCAD, his practice quickly evolved into a means of exploring socio-political anomalies locally and internationally, utilising his creativity to ask questions, never shying away from political controversy and always striving for solutions to divisive social-issues that have affected him throughout his life. After graduating, Euan went on to work in a local prison as a Peer Support Worker, Recovery Coach and Art Therapist, using his own Lived Experience as a catalyst to help encourage prisoners at their lowest points to take the first few steps towards recovery. By attending art workshops that enable them to begin to process any personal or social issues that have brought them to this point in life and by using their creativity as an outlet to work through these problems, prisoners can then move on to the SMART Recovery program where they can attend "Self-Management and Recovery Training". Education and Lived Experience has always gone hand-in-hand for Euan, so while working in the prison he continued his studies on the MFA Fine course at DJCAD, where he aims to progress to PhD level so that he can research, write and create art that focuses on the links between addiction, psychology and creativity; and the importance of peer learning in recovery. In parallel, he collaborates with the prison to discover new ways to improve recidivism rates for criminals with substance misuse issues.

Euan was a recipient of the 2022 InGEAR Publishing Awards.

If you wish to support Euan or want to follow his journey, please feel free to contact... Email – euanrutter@hotmail.co.uk Instagram - @euanrutter.art Blog - http://forthewarofart.wordpress.com.

Abstract

Posthumanism, "The critical perspective that the age of humanism has come to an end" (Wolfe, 2022) is here and times are changing fast but as artists, what can we do to shape the future of the world when artificial intelligence is threatening to overtake humanity and bring an end to the Anthropocene, the period in which humanity has had a detrimental ecological impact on the planet . During the recent coronavirus pandemic a digital integration has been occurring, as we have lived hermetic existences that were heavily dependent on technology to interact with the world around us. In this dissertation, the aim is to explore the circumstances that have brought us to this moment in history and ask questions of the digital developments that are shaping our future, the implications and dangers of these changes, how it will affect us artists and creatives, and how we can adapt to this technological transformation to continue to positively impact human culture.

Euan Rutter

Introduction

Now then, we find ourselves in quite the cultural predicament and it would seem there is an imminent need for change as our little planetary rock hurtles towards a species-altering dilemma, which manifests itself in post-humanist theory and is engineered by the influence of artificial intelligence (AI). Technology is at the forefront of these developments and is grossly prevalent in society already today so to imagine a future entirely dictated by computer algorithms, combined with the introduction of human symbiosis with machine, augmented and in an interplanetary environment, is not too difficult to understand - even more so if you have ever watched or read any science fiction material.

Posthumanism is a multi-disciplined ideal that explores the possibilities of what it will mean for humanity when we reach a state of becoming "beyond-human" and by doing so it attempts to imagine how the world may look in a future where we have reached a point of cultural advancement via our integration with AI. This is very similar to the Transhumanist movement that hopes to go one step further and download consciousness into a synthetic organism before discarding of its human remains.

Will we still be human? Are we already "Posthuman?" To be able to understand the underlying currents behind such theories, we must firstly understand the notions that precede the concept and the humanist ideologies that inspired the Renaissance movement, why this still influences modern times, and how it relates to the present topic. We must weigh it up against the comparisons of the world nowadays, as we brace ourselves for a new utopian future imagined by tech giants and billionaire colonialists such as Bill Gates (Microsoft), Jeff Bezos (Amazon) and Elon Musk (Tesla).

The human advancement in belief and consciousness which transcended during the Renaissance period saw a momentous surge in artistic and cultural endeavours, epitomised by historical works from the likes of Leonardo

An artist's perspective of posthumanism and AI

Da Vinci (1452-1519), Michelangelo (1475-1564), Raphael (1483-1520), and Caravaggio (1571-1610) - each attaining a legendary level of craftmanship in an era still celebrated today as the birth of the classical arts, but this cultural shift also came at a cost and with blood on its hands... the blood of colonial conquests that aimed to spread the ideology of a rejuvenated Western society which devoured everything in its path, changing the course of history forever.

> *They always say time changes things, but you actually have to change them yourself. Progress is impossible without change, and those who cannot change their minds cannot change anything. If we don't change, we don't grow. If we don't grow, we aren't really living.*
>
> *- Aristotle 384 BC – 322 AD*

Greek philosopher Aristotle explains to us that time itself cannot change our reality but instead, that it is down to us to affect that change within ourselves – firstly, because if we cannot accomplish this, then we shall never grow, we will never attain our full potential and we will never really be truly alive. Fast forward to these modern times and it is now a concept that echoes eerily in the distance but is still as applicable today as it was back then, where we are charted on course to a technological singularity that will question our very humanity and seek to achieve the proposed metamorphic advancement needed to fully usher in the posthuman/transhuman phase of our evolutionary process.

To change often is to be perfect. Such an ideology could be applied to any scenario or dilemma, from the minor issues like my art practice to the anthropocentric conundrum we are experiencing today but the theory is exceptionally adept in relation to issues like the global warming crisis, overpopulation, and the need to secure a sustainable future. But how these changes may come into realisation is not elementary for you, nor I, but for the billionaire colonialists and corporations who are leading the charge ahead into the future with innovations that are ready to combine man and machine. These aspire for us to be living in utopian colonies, and have some even predicting the possibility that immortality is now on the table.

An artist's perspective of posthumanism and AI

These topics have been the focus of many renowned writers, philosophers, and artists over the years, and the echoes of the Renaissance period still leave a lot to be explored - but my aim for the moment is to help you to better understand the moral, cultural, and philosophical repercussions of these crusades of enlightenment and the colonial consequences of aggressive capitalist progression so that we can begin to discuss how artists can adapt to the situation, as the world experiences a shunt into further digital dependence and how we can move forward into the future - in acknowledgement, that change is an inevitably not to be feared but to be embraced.

Posthumanism has recently been a growing area of important research, as demonstrated by a search of the British Library's thesis collection (see for example, Wilde 2016, Chkhaidz 2021 and Wilson Hughes 2021) but there is no significant research into how artists can navigate the coming developments, nor on how this transition can be achieved, to ensure that we can continue to positively influence any shift in culture. Although, the area has been written and researched extensively by many before myself, there appears to be a significant gap in knowledge that needs to be addressed sooner rather than later - so it is my intention to further explore these issues in the hope of presenting a platform for future scholarly activity.

The research and ideas that will be discussed directly affect my own art practice, as technology has been integrated into my work during the past year of coronavirus lockdowns. However, it has also further enhanced my creative dexterity so therefore, my own ideas of being an artist have already been severely affected. There had to be an adaptation to the transformations presented before us, and we will soon learn that disruption is the key to change.

As artists prepare for the end of their studies and step into professional practice, the drive towards digital integration has become overbearingly apparent, which at times has left me questioning my practice because times are changing, the arts are changing and the need for artists are changing. With the recent trend of digital arts and non-fungible tokens (NFTs), creatives at all levels have been put on notice that the traditional arts days of glory and dominance may be at an end, as crypto gets cultural.

Chapter one

Back to the Future

To be able to understand the complexity and indeed the necessity for humanity to take this fool's leap forward and the next "superhuman" evolutionary step is by no means a small feat because it is a multiverse of a concept that needs time to digest. However, together we can explore these themes and begin to decipher what is being forecast so that we may garner a better understanding of the morality and of the consequences of our posthuman advancement - but also - so that I personally may use this information to begin to charter my own path into an exceedingly uncertain future for contemporary artists. In particularly, there have been recent announcements of cuts to government funding for the arts in the United Kingdom and the surge in the demand for technologically adept creatives, as discussed by Gareth Harris (2021) in an article for *The Art Newspaper*.

But before we get into that, let us have a look at the current events unfolding and begin to lay down the bones of what the main catalysts are for such an outlandish and altogether disturbing theory, and begin to dissect the remnants of the anthropocentric corpse that has been laid bare on the operating table, patiently waiting for us to assess the damage so we can learn where we went wrong.

The evolution of humanity has since time age-old been propelled by the discovery of new information and technologies, from the humble beginnings of homo-erectus with his tool making and the discovery of fire, to the present era of artificial intelligence and space exploration. The ingenuity and innovation of the brightest minds over the generations has transformed the destiny of our race with seismic shifts in the belief systems that have defined our evolutionary process - by not only radically altering how we view ourselves culturally, but how we view ourselves in the cosmological schematic of which we represent a miniscule proportion.

An artist's perspective of posthumanism and AI

Humanism and the anthropocentric train of thought were born from the belief that people were central to destiny of the universe, with a divine right to reign superior over all other creatures on the earth because we had developed a mind and consciousness that separated man from beast. But with this newfound self-awareness we became spiritual beings that attempted to set up (or re-establish, if you are so inclined), a connection to the interdimensional source and origin of our existence, whether this has been through religion, spirituality, or more recently, science - it is a desire that has been strived for consistently over the generations.

> *Both humanism and its modern antithesis, posthumanism, originated in the western hemisphere. In Renaissance Europe, Christianity was the central concept driving art, but to it was added the force of humanism—a new and popular philosophy that originated in the late 1400s. Humanism caught on because its focus on human potential coincided with the rise of Europeans' sense of their own power, as both scholars and seafarers from its countries began to uncover*

> *new territory. Ironically, despite growing scepticism about the science of ancient Greece and Rome, humanism started with the fifteenth-century rediscovery of some mystical texts from the classical era.*
>
> *- la Grandeur (n.d.)*

Throughout history every single civilization and culture has expressed a belief that a higher power was the architect of all life on earth. The discovery of Cabalistic Hebrew texts, Eastern mysticism, and ancient scriptures by the Western Christian world, foretold that God-like powers could be attained by performing elaborately archaic and occult practices, in a remarkably similar tale to the ego trips experienced by tech giants and their discovery of new technologies.

We now have an understanding of where this inflated self of sense began to arise, while simultaneously fueling the egotistical and empirical ambitions of European Christians with the belief that they were the true sole representatives of Gods power on Earth. Even still to this day the Pope keeps this divinatory mantle as the one true connection between the civilized world and the astral plane from where creation emanates - or some other obscure version of that theory. With such an illustrious and virtuoso position of responsibility, I sincerely hope he is well compensated for the personal sacrifices he has made in the name of his calling.

This change in thinking that peaked with the Renaissance period, famed for its ascension in the arts that inspired and celebrated this newly held humanist belief of introverted divination, was with no shadow of a doubt a turning point for civilization. Consequently, it also preceded the quest for colonial domination in the name of spreading Christianity to every corner of the known world, carving its scar upon history, as we continue to come to terms with the influences and afflictions it still inflicts upon society today - fascism, racism, colonialism, bigotry, geographical and financial inequality.

Fast forward to the present and the post-humanist conundrum, and we have an altogether different scenario that still brandishes all the hallmarks of the movement it claims to be the antithesis of but for vastly distinct reasons.

Much like humanism, we are currently experiencing the early onset of a cultural shift that has been brought about by the discovery of new information and technologies, that are opening new doorways and challenge the perceptions of what it means to be a human and what we will be capable of. Instead of being inspired by ancient mysticism and writings, technology and artificial intelligence are the catalysts that are now recharting the course for the transformation of our existence.

These similarities are incongruently haunting and something not to be ignored because if we want to break free from the anthropocentric way of thinking that bares the wounds of past failures, then we must learn some very harsh lessons from the past so that we do not continue to make the same mistakes in the future, by repeating the same destructive patterns that have failed to serve us historically for a more equal, fairer and more prosperous society for all.

For example, let us consider the apocalyptic global warming crisis that can be attributed to the pollution stemming forward from the industrial revolution to the present day, irreparably damaging the ozone layer and driven by capitalism, and mass consumerism. This is the world we live in, and it is corrupt to the core because we are struggling to disassociate with the mindset that continues to support the societal inequalities and prejudices that sees people still being persecuted and marginalised currently by control structures that are deeply entrenched in humanist tradition and privilege (Curtis, 2022).

This has brought us to the present stage where our governments and corporations have become divisive entities that have no interest in influencing effective change because they prefer to instead pursue the destructive capitalist system that has brought them their wealth and power. They proclaim that the complexities of world economics are too intertwined and fragile to be unravelled so they cling to the belief that this is the only way the entire system can function without collapsing. They are probably right, but only in as much so that they would stand to lose their substantial grip on wealth, power, influence and control (Curtis, 2022).

It is a virtual panopticon of a reality we have found ourselves in and because of it we will always struggle to break free from the will of those in power, and completely sever ties entirely with the humanist thinking that has corrupted the modern world because by the very nature of it, it will continue to reborn and, in doing so will be inherently incorporated into the new and shiny posthuman world - not just as a relic – instead, as the nucleus for the rebirthing of civilization.

This idea has been explored previously in the paper 'Theorising Humanism' by Neil Badmington (2003), as he discusses the works of many humanists, anti-humanists and postmodern philosophers, as they themselves were exploring the possibilities of the posthuman era. In particular, I would like to share with you an excerpt from his analysis of French writer, Jacques Derrida (1930-2004), who was an immensely influential philosopher in the fields of post-modernism and post-structuralism:

> *Deconstruction, rather, as he has insisted on various occasions, consists in repeating things in a certain way, in order to expose the overwhelming uncertainty of even the most*

An artist's perspective of posthumanism and AI

> *apparently certain discourses. If the version of posthumanism that I am trying to develop here repeats humanism, it does so in a certain way and with a view to the deconstruction of anthropocentric thought. If the pure out- side is a myth, it is nonetheless possible to lodg[e] oneself within traditional conceptuality in order to destroy it.*
>
> – Badmington 2003

Derrida tells us that Deconstruction, the theory that explores the phenomena of why we do not know how to explain what we know, is a concept that can be adapted to societal changes, or lack thereof. The possibility of change is being low-balled by world leaders and their lack of ambition to seek a significant break in the traditions of old because they do so in the hope that humanity will inevitably repeat and re-invent itself consistently within the set parameters of an anthropocentric viewpoint.

So, what we should be focusing on with posthumanism is not an apocalyptic ending for humankind or an ascension to a technological singularity that we should be concerned with but instead, on how we can achieve an end to the destructive anthropocentric mindset, while we make the transformation by growing from within it - much like Badmington (b.1971) has been discussing before us.

There needs to be an autopsy of the humanist corpse to see what it is worth salvaging and what can be improved upon, but more importantly, that it takes heed of the warnings from past failures and incubates a positive rebirthing in post-humanist theory. Here we might move forward in harmony and set out the welcome mat for the consciousness shift that we will purportedly achieve. So, in moving ahead with human advancement, we must be extremely cautious where we dare to tread because history is most certainly not on our side and we cannot afford to make the same mistakes again (Badmington, 2003).

The death of the anthropocene is an unavoidable inevitability and we will soon be ushered forward into a new dawn and a new era, but the question is... with the added influence of corrupt politicians, tech billionaires and colonial corporations leading the way forward, and in tandem with an artificial intelligence already driving our culture, consistently improving every year by up to fifty percent in power and scale, one might ask, where exactly are we headed with all this knowledge and posthuman technology? We shall explore this further in the following chapters by looking at the innovations and concepts that are being proposed to us for a brighter and more sustainable future.

Euan Rutter

Chapter 2

Looking Into the Beyond

As you are reading this there is a great likelihood that you will be doing so on an electronic device because this is the method by which we are increasingly consuming information in the modern era and almost every single one of you will be carrying around an electronic device on your person at all times to either communicate with friends and family, for work purposes, for banking, storing personal information or data, to read news and watch films.

The rapid recent advancements in technology have been so vast that nearly everyone on the planet is now connected, whether that be on a mobile phone, computer or games console. The population has never been quite so interlinked before and people quite literally have a world of information at their fingertips. This in retrospect is a reflection of human symbiosis with artificial intelligence in its current state and it is furthermore, a precursor of what is to come in the not-too-distant future.

We have become dependent on these technologies to structure the very fabric of our existence and societal structures. They have been integrated into every aspect of our daily lives and they know everything about us - but what do we know of them? The corporations and shady figures in control of these companies have become more powerful than countries. Their influence on world affairs has become extremely questionable and their capitalist ideologies leave a lot to be desired (Clement, 2006). They are not exactly the most reputable of characters and their businesses have been linked to an array of misdemeanours and scandals linked to privacy concerns, the collection and illegal sale of personal information and data, tax evasion and the exploitation of lower-class workers - and that's just the business side of things (Taschner, 2022).

More importantly though, they are exclusively, all the very same tech billionaires that are proposing the numerous fantastical utopian colonies on earth and in the stars, and the race is definitely on as several notable names like Bill Gates, Mark Zuckerberg and Marc Lore, have been buying up hundreds of thousands of acres of uninhabited desert territories in places like Arizona, USA. Jeff Bezos, Elon Musk and Richard Branson also have their respective quests to conquer space and the final frontier.

This is a major concern that has also been investigated by writer, Jessa Crispin, in her article for *The Guardian* (2021), in which she discusses the plans by the owner of Walmart Marc Lore, to develop a city of the future, an eco-friendly utopian metropolis filled with avant-garde architecture and communal resources - named, Telosa, in the Arizona desert. Coincidentally, it also comes complete with its very own futuristic monorail, reminiscent of the Simpsons episode in which an eccentric salesman swindles the town into paying for a death ride of a transport system and then runs off with their money (Groening, 1993).

> *Watching all this, it almost makes sense that someone with the means and the desire to help might want to take a more direct route. And the ideas*

of this fake little town are grand! Green architecture, environmental technology, transparent governance, innovative urban planning ideas – if this works, it could advance our thinking on how humans can exist in a changing world and live harmonious lives during the coming environmental and economic calamities.

It won't work because one guy doesn't get to decide how the world, or even a city, should work. Even if he's collaborating with the greatest thinkers and architects and scientists of our time, just a glance through Lore's portfolio will reveal that all of his big ideas and fancy language about the betterment and advancement of society are pretty hollow –

Crispin, 2021

Crispin, above, bluntly tells us in no uncertain terms that it would not work and more importantly, should not, under any circumstances, be allowed to be single-handedly decided by people like Lore because of his reputation from Walmart for exploitative business practices and the connections to other corporations with shocking treatment of workers – such as Amazon, who paid him $545 million, for the acquisition of his new venture, Diapers.com.

Euan Rutter

Chapter 3

Into the Matrix

Techno-scientists are yet to map the exact path of the future of human life as AI is increasingly impacting it. In the words of Klaus Schwab, an industry spokesperson whose position reveals the influential role of commercial interests in driving research in this field, 'We do not yet know just how it will unfold (but) when compared with previous industrial revolutions, the Fourth is evolving at an exponential rather than a linear pace'.

However, since Vernor Vinge's NASA paper, 'The coming technological Singularity, how to survive in the posthuman era' (1993), a consensus is that the nadir point of the revolution in artificial intelligence will be marked by a convergence of capabilities drawn from machine learning and neuroscience into a fusion of the operative power of the computer with that of the human brain, a aingularity (Clark and Chalmers 1998; Russell and Novig 2009, pp.13–15).

In the paper 'The future of artificial intelligence, posthumanism and the infection of Pixley Isaka Seme's African humanism' by Malesela John Lamola, the concept of fusing together computers and human beings is described as somewhat of an inevitability and it will see the arrival of the much-hyped technological singularity, the point in which there is no return, when technological advancement will be out of control and any subsequential changes on our civilisation will be irreversible. Although, what I personally find most worrying is the investment from corporate enterprises and their involvement in any research projects which tap into the framework of the cerebral cortex with artificial intelligence.

The integration of people and technology has up until now been an almost exclusively superficial process or so we might initially believe, but when we think about such medical procedures that require pacemakers, prosthetics, hearing aids and such, the advances in medical science are

An artist's perspective of posthumanism and AI

already prolonging and improving lives and wellbeing. However, it is also due to augmentation with artificial intelligence, this is happening now, so what else is to be expected in a future when upgrading your hardware becomes no more than a cosmetic procedure? Well... for the first time, now we will discuss the ingenuity of the eccentric protagonist of the future, Elon Musk (b.1971).

You may have heard about the controversial 'Neuralink' programme being developed by Musk and his associates, who are working on a chip that can be intravenously inserted directly into the brain and connect to the neural network that controls the electrical pulses sent and received by receptors. Statements suggest that patients suffering from degenerative neurological diseases such as parkinson's disease, motor neurone disease and cerebral palsy, to name but a few, may soon be able to restore lost brain function (Gopal Vasishta, 2022; Fadziso, 2020).

Initially, the nanochips will attach themselves to blood cells to circulate but they will eventually be minute enough to breach the brain/blood barrier, thus allowing us to begin to manipulate the brain chemistry that controls our motor functions such as mobility, behaviours, impulses and emotions (Gopal Vasishta, 2022). These are sceptical developments that claim the possibility of super-longevity by increasing life expectancy with a view to one day achieving immortality.

While sounding like a genuine attempt to cure the degenerative brain diseases that affect millions of people, at what point will the developments stop? As we are fully well aware, these technologies will continue to improve and become more effective over time so what we must ask is - what would be the next steps in the process when they are already training monkeys to play games using only brainpower? (Wakefield, 2022). Planet of the Apes springs to mind primarily but let us just consider only humans and what they might have in store for us.

There is a possibility that the Neuralink chip may go on to cure other illnesses caused by chemical imbalances in the brain that cause depression or ADHD to mention a couple. It may introduce the ability to stream music directly into your head without the need for headphones or any other external audio device, or going deeper still, being able to download new skills without having to spend months learning new languages - programming or martial arts - just like in the movie trilogy The Matrix (1999), where Keanu Reeves is plugged into the system and endowed with super-human abilities.

Symbiosis with technology is the end goal and there is no limit to what can be achieved but at this stage the morality of the situation comes into question because at what point will we no longer be a human being and start to become a cybernetic organism? With a computer for a mind that has eradicated any negative or defective thoughts and brain functions... void of human error? A fine-tuned mind controlling an organic body appears ideal but when you remove the ability to make mistakes, we risk losing our individuality because is it not so that because of our flaws, it is that which make us who we are?

Euan Rutter

Chapter 4

Without Purpose

Since the beginning of the industrial revolution, technology and machinery has been developed to boost the levels of production, manufacturing and commerce, but it has come at the cost of generations of workers who have found themselves surplus to requirements and out of work as their trades were replaced by autonomous creations that were void of human error. This is a trend that has continued to spike over the decades as new innovations such as the printing press, steam engines and more recently the computer, that has revolutionised the world around us and has brought us to this point of advancement.

In the TEDxYYC talk, 'Preparing for a future with Artificial Intelligence', Robin Winsor explains to us that there will come a time in the future when machines replace humans entirely and in every role. This a very audacious statement and one that may be true nonetheless because the evidence is there for all to see with the invention of self-driving vehicles, like the Tesla cars also developed by Mr Musk, the operation of drones and the automation of factories, warehouses and distribution centres, already proving that human input is not a necessity.

So, what will become of us when we are no longer fit for the purposes of employment? How will we cope with our own existence without purpose or direction in our lives? With so many people nowadays defined by what they do for a living and the insistence of capitalism and consumerism dictating the societal order of the Western world to the point where people have become slaves to a power structure that strenuously dangles the golden carrot of fortune beyond us - how can we move forward in a world where we have nothing to aim for and nothing to gain, and how will the differential in equality be affected if we are all equal in stature and social standing?

Winsor then goes on to discuss how this change of belief in our earthly purpose will give us the opportunity to explore the things that bring us joy - our hobbies, pastimes and the personal ambitions that we hold dearest so we can attain self-fulfilment. For artists this sounds like it should be an amazing prospect, and that would give us the opportunity to develop our creative passions and dedicate all our time and resources to achieving greatly expressive works that might spark off our own new-age renaissance.

This newfound freedom to pursue our dreams should also fuel a wave of super well-being for humanity and usher in an era of peace and happiness, a utopian ideology that is difficult to understand given the current situation worldwide and the gap between the richest and poorest sections of society being stretched further than ever before. However, it is one that comes straight from the playbooks of posthumanism and transhumanism, the movement 'which advocates the enhancement of the human condition by developing and making widely available sophisticated technologies able to greatly enhance longevity, mood, and cognitive abilities, and predicts the emergence of such technologies in the future' (Transhumanism - Wikipedia, 2022).

Euan Rutter

Chapter 5

Where Art Thou?

Artists that explore the posthuman genre usually try to imagine the physical changes that we will undergo when we become beyond human but what interests me most is what will become of artists during this transition? They say art imitates life and vice versa, so when these changes begin to manifest themselves, artists must also evolve alongside them because for centuries we have helped shape the world around us and just like the Renaissance artists before us, we are striving to create a vision of where we are going by looking to the past for inspiration and guidance (Why is the Renaissance important? – ItalianRenaissance.org, 2022).

The arts have changed dramatically over the past few decades with the invention of innovative technologies that allow for creative expression to be further explored with the release of new software and programs being made available to us. For example, throughout the pandemic students worldwide were given unlimited free access to Adobe Creative Suite and other 3D design software to continue being creative, but for over the past twenty plus years there has been a surge in non-traditional artists creating quite a storm in the art world - currently none more so than the posthuman posterchild who has thrown the whole establishment into meltdown.

Last year, at the height of the pandemic, there were the shock headlines and introduction of Non-Fungible Tokens (NFTs) and 3D artists, specifically Mike Winkelman aka Beeple, who broke auction house records with the sale of his NFT 'Everydays: The First 5000 Days', in which he had continuously developed a new digital artwork every day for 13 years using a range of digital techniques in Maya, Blender, Adobe Photoshop and After Effects - gradually progressing further to achieve some notable and politically charged results along the way.

An artist's perspective of posthumanism and AI

What is most significant about the sale of his work is that the appearance of NFTs have revolutionised the way that art can be bought and owned digitally because up until this point digital art was difficult to sell, because there was no way of truly knowing if the work was original or of verifying the artists ownership rights. However, with technology advancing the way it does, it was not long until someone came up with a solution based on the blockchain used by cryptocurrencies. This allows artwork to be minted onto the network and, thus verifies the authenticity and origin of the artist making the sale.

Of course, digital art is not a new media and has been explored by many other artists who have used the availability of modern technology to create art and push the envelope of what is possible with the use of artificial intelligence. For example, John Gerard, the Irish artist, began exploring 3D scanning and photography as a means of creating virtual sculptures, which are finally displayed using Real-Time computer graphics. Technology is a key factor in Gerard's work and by using the same methods found in creating video games he can take thousands of digital pictures that can be integrated into creating new landscapes that are extremely realistic but entirely imaginary.

Gerard's transient work, a 'Thousand Year Dawn (Marcel)' (2005), is one such work that is extremely realistic, but it is in fact a computer simulation that shows a man watching the sunset. Although the sun is programmed to set over the course of a thousand-year period it seems that it is not moving at all but that is because it has been programmed to happen in real-time so seeing the work in its entirety is impossible. The concept is simple, but it begins to show the possibilities available to visual artists when we introduce technology into the equation.

As I have journeyed through the latter phase of my art school journey, focus has shifted on to professional practice and where it may lead to in the future, which has left me pondering what roles there are for artists in this new world that we are creating, and it has been a disorientating process to say the least because my work has taken on an entirely digital format. This has opened many new door ways for my practice, which became apparent as I began to explore

An artist's perspective of posthumanism and AI

digital collage, animation, publication, 3D design and creative coding, as additional means of creativity.

Although, it has been an enlightening experience of the skills needed to break into the digital creative industries, admittedly, I have become extremely conscious of the digital intervention that we are experiencing and the reasoning behind it because as we know, it was not just an issue that had affected the creative industry of course but also every other area of business, commerce and public services too. What were the intentions of this push, who was behind it and more specifically, who was profiting from it?

Author Naomi Klein has written several books over the past decade or so, most notably *No Logo, This Changes Everything* and in particular, *The Shock Doctrine: The Rise of Disaster Capitalism*. This text investigates and discusses the underlying parasitical ideologies that are found deeply entrenched within the thoughts of neoconservative capitalists, politicians and corporations, who religiously follow the radical economic policies left behind as a legacy by Milton Friedman. What we are left with is their aggressive pursuit of free markets and trade without government regulation (see for example, Klein 2007).

In a recent interview, Klein goes on to discuss the current coronavirus situation and how 'Big Tech' companies have profited from the crisis, but furthermore makes connections to the patterns that have been evolving over the past thirty years, where corporate colonialists have been capitalising on some of the worst social and economic disasters like the 9/11 attacks, the Iraq war, Hurricane Katrina and numerous other conflicts and crises. This is a sentiment that was also explored in a recent *New York Times* article, 'How Big Tech Won the Pandemic' (2021), where Shira Ovide explores how they managed to generate so much wealth in a short space of time.

> *In the last year, the five tech superpowers — Amazon, Apple, Google, Microsoft and Facebook — had combined revenue of more than $1.2 trillion, as I wrote for The Times on Thursday. It was a strange and amazing year for Big Tech. I can't believe it, but some of the companies*

> *are growing faster and are more profitable than they have been in years. The pandemic has made the tech giants and their bosses unfathomably rich (even more unfathomably rich than they were before).*
>
> *– Ovide, S (2021)*

This is a sentiment echoed in the recent paper 'Virtual Architecture, Art, Pandemic, Protest', in which the author explores the inequalities brought to light during the pandemic, the further plunge into digital dependence and how we can challenge the onslaught of divisive capitalist progressions in the future (Gilbert, 2022).

Ovide goes on tell us that during the pandemic, companies like Google, Facebook and Amazon took advantage of strange circumstances to force smaller businesses, who were to struggling to stay open, to adapt to using their platforms so that they could continue to operate. The world went online, leading to the sale of computers, software, programs and other digital devices going through the roof, as everyone from business to education and beyond now worked from home and in the process of doing so, further stretched the deficit between wealthiest and the poorest.

As socially-conscious creatures, artists have been challenging these problems for many years (Upton-Hansen et al., 2020) but as time progresses, the lines between art and digital art have consistently intertwined and we have also become dependent on these technological progressions, leaving us with a moment for moral reflection, before we further adapt to the emigration towards a cyber future (Sobrinho and Silva, 2018). We must begin to become more aware of our obligation to mankind to continue to challenge the autonomous organisations and corporations who are paving the way forward for humanity with visions of eco-friendly utopias, human symbiosis with AI and space colonialism, built at the expense of the lower-class workers they exploit by paying minimum wages and the anthropocentric damage they have caused to the environment.

Conclusion

The artist's task is to save the soul of mankind; and anything less is a dithering while Rome burns. Because of the artists, who are self-selected, for being able to journey into the Other, if the artists cannot find the way, then the way cannot be found.

– McKenna, 1995

To begin to bring this book to its conclusion I have included a quote by author, eco-activist and psychedelic explorer, Terence McKenna, as he gives us his view during a filmed interview before his passing. He explains that the role of artists is to 'save the soul of mankind'. We can help imagine, influence and shape a better future, uncorrupted by aggressive capitalists and eccentric billionaires because he believed that through art we can grow and transcend the changes that lie ahead.

We have previously discussed the writings of Badmington and his theory that to bring an end to the anthropocentric ideology which has gradually brought the world to its knees. The purpose is not to abandon it completely but to take what good is left and recreate a better version of it. Posthumanism is not just a nightmarish vision of the future but an opportunity for us to grow ourselves so that we can be part of the change, just like the great Aristotle proclaimed over two thousand years ago when he told us that to keep changing is to be perfect.

The gauntlet has been thrown down to artists and creatives to help reimagine and rebuild society in times when Big Tech is rebuilding the world that they helped to destroy. La Grandeur told us that artists were celebrated as the ones who shaped the Humanism movement and of the repercussions of the last time there was a seismic cultural shift of this magnitude, and the warning signs are there so art must become the antitheses of the destructive capitalist ideology shaping the future, as we progress into a new era

An artist's perspective of posthumanism and AI

because if we don't, it will be left to the devices of a select few egomaniacs.

This brings me back to the foul-mouthed Mike Winkleman aka Beeple, because although he is the poster-boy of the recent shock NFT developments causing a stir in the art world, he is also a prime example of a 3D digital artist who uses his platform and fame to challenge Big Tech, corrupt politicians and their grandiose exploits, in a way that demonstrates how we can adapt to the changes and continue to oppose the exploitation from within - just like the seed of humanism growing within womb of posthumanism.

The development of new technologies that allow artists and designers to expand their creative abilities digitally has opened up a multitude of possibilities for what can be achieved with the use of artificial intelligence to create art. Take for example, the introduction of creative coding and the possibility of being able to draw by writing a program that will do it for you - or being able to create visual art installations by creating code that can make light and audio interactive with the viewer.

In this particular example, there are literally millions of possibilities that can be achieved and furthermore, learning the necessary code and syntax needed to create generative art, gives artists an opportunity to learn the basic understanding of writing the programming languages that are used to control almost every aspect of technology. This may seem like a daunting process for most but given the trajectory we are on, towards digital symbiosis ,it might be a useful skill to be familiar with in the event of a posthuman Renaissance.

During the past few months, creative coding is something that I began to experiment with and had some positive results, gaining a lot of new knowledge in learning the basic commands needed to generate a generative image in an app called Processing, designed by Casey Reas and Ben Fry. These scholars used their knowledge to collaborate with a group of artists, designers, developers and programmers, to create a software that is designed to be able to help and encourage creatives to learn how to code.

Processing is just a starting point before moving on to more complicated techniques, but what has interested me most in my research of the programme is that in the development stages, the reason behind bringing together both artists and programmers is because they have numerous similarities in their approach to their practice – we are methodical in process, analytical in execution and we use the same creative problem-solving patterns.

When they collaborated with one another it was beneficial for both sides because the artists and designers would learn how to programme and create generative visual art, while the developers would learn valuable design aspects that vastly improved the visual aesthetic of the programmes and games they had been working on.

Which begs the question… if funding for arts education is being drastically slashed in favour of STEM research subjects, then why is programming, and other digital arts for that matter, not being introduced into arts educations at secondary school, college and university levels? This would encourage young creatives to consider coding and digital arts, as an extension or as an alternative artistic media that offers a multitude of opportunities in moving forward into professional creative practice.

If programming could be adapted as a creative outlet that gives artists an opportunity to learn computer language, then it is possible that given the most extreme predictions for the future, then this may well be the trojan horse needed to transcend the posthuman advancements from within the system - but then again, we may not need to worry, we are after all in capable hands… right?

References

Art's Task Is To Save The Soul Of Mankind | Terence McKenna (Shared 2019) www.youtube.com. Available at: https://www.youtube.com/watch?v=QDA9_N4vxpg (Accessed: 15 October 2021).

Artuner.com. (2021). John Gerard. [online] Available at: https://www.artuner.com/wp-content/uploads/John-Gerrard-1.pdf. [Accessed 7 October 2021].

Ayhan, N. (no date) .Renaissance and Humanism. www.academia.edu. Available at: https://www.academia.edu/10416041/Renaissance_and_Humanism (Accessed: 18 May 2021).

Badmington, N. (2003). Theorizing Posthumanism. Cultural Critique. (53), 10-27. (Accessed: 22 March 2021) Available at: http://www.jstor.org/stable/1354622

Chkhaidze, I. (2021). Posthumanism in the works of Patricia Piccinini, Matthew Barney and Charles Avery. [online] Ethos.bl.uk. Available at: https://ethos.bl.uk/OrderDetails.do?uin=uk.bl.ethos.666797 . [Accessed 18 October 2021].

Clement, W., 2006. Corporate Power in a Globalizing World: A Study in Elite Social Organization (review). The Canadian Journal of Sociology, [online] 31(1), pp.146-148. Available at: https://muse.jhu.edu/article/196577/summary [Accessed 11 January 2022].

Coope, U., 2005. Time for Aristotle: Physics IV. 10-14. 1st ed. Oxford: Oxford University Press, p.71.

Crispin, J., 2021. A billionaire wants to build a utopia in the US desert. Seems like this could go wrong | Jessa Crispin. [online] the Guardian. Available at: https://www.theguardian.com/commentisfree/2021/sep/20/a-billionaire-wants-to-build-a-utopia-in-the-us-desert-seems-like-this-could-go-wrong [Accessed 11 October 2021].

Curtis, A., 2022. Can't Get You Out of My Head. [online] BBC iPlayer. Available at: https://www.bbc.co.uk/iplayer/episodes/p093wp6h/cant-get-you-out-of-my-head [Accessed 24 January 2022].

En.wikipedia.org. 2022. Transhumanism - Wikipedia. [online] Available at: https://en.wikipedia.org/wiki/Transhumanism [Accessed 4 January 2022].

Fadziso, T., 2020. https://iiste.org/Journals/index.php/ADS/article/view/52906. Arts and Design Studies, [online] 7(1). Available at: https://i-proclaim.my/journals/index.php/ajhal/article/view/518 [Accessed 24 January 2021].

Groening, M., 1993. The Simpsons 4x12 "Marge vs. the Monorail". [online] Trakt. Available at: https://trakt.tv/shows/the-simpsons/seasons/4/episodes/12 [Accessed 24 January 2022].

Harris, G., 2021(2021) UK government approves 50% funding cut for arts and design courses. [online] The Art Newspaper - International art news and events. Available at: https://www.theartnewspaper.com/2021/07/22/uk-government-approves-50percent-funding-cut-for-arts-and-design-courses [Accessed 6 October 2021].

Kastrenakes, J. (2021). Beeple sold an NFT for $69 million. [online] The Verge. Available at: https://www.theverge.com/2021/3/11/22325054/beeple-christies-nft-sale-cost-everydays-69-million. [Accessed 2 October 2021].

Klein, N (2021) Big Tech and the Pandemic. [online] www.youtube.com. Available at: https://youtu.be/17XWaLV6C8c (Accessed 12 October 2021).

Klein, N., 2010. The Shock Doctrine. 1st ed. [Metropolitan Books]: Henry Holt and Co.

Lagrandeur, K. and Professor (no date) Posthumanism and Contemporary Art. Available at: https://www.mocacleveland.org/sites/default/files/files/lagrandeurpaperfinal.pdf (Accessed: 22 March 2021).

Lamola, M. (2020) The future of artificial intelligence, posthumanism and the infection of Pixley Isaka Seme's African humanism. (Accessed17/07/2021) available at: The_future_of_artificial_intelligence_po.pdf

Morton, T. (2016) Ecology Without Nature. [Website] CCCB LAB. Available at: https://lab.cccb.org/en/tim-morton-ecology-without-nature/ [Accessed: 22 March 2021].

Our Post-Human Future. | David Simpson | TEDxSantoDomingo (no date) www.youtube.com. Available at: Our Post-Human Future | David Simpson | TEDxSantoDomingo [Accessed: 22 March 2021].

Ovide, S. (2021). How Big Tech Won the Pandemic. [online] Nytimes.com.

Available at: https://www.nytimes.com/2021/04/30/technology/big-tech-pandemic.html [Accessed 18 October 2021].

Peterson, C., 2021. Monkey Trouble: The Scandal of Posthumanism. [online] JSTOR. Available at: https://www.jstor.org/stable/j.ctt1xhr5xz [Accessed 1 October 2021].

Posthumanism and Contemporary Art. | Widewalls (no date) www.widewalls.ch. Available at: https://www.widewalls.ch/magazine/posthumanism-contemporary-art

Preparing for a future with Artificial Intelligence. | Robin Winsor | TEDxYYC (no date) www.youtube.com. Available at: Preparing for a future with Artificial Intelligence | Robin Winsor | TEDxYYC [Accessed: 22 March 2021].

Sky News. 2022. Bezos, Branson, and Musk: What you need to know about the billionaire space race. [online] Available at: https://news.sky.com/story/bezos-branson-musk-the-new-space-race-explained-as-virgin-galactic-prepares-to-launch-12347249 [Accessed 6 January 2022].

Taschner, J., 2022. About | HeinOnline. [online] HeinOnline. Available at: https://heinonline.org/HOL/LandingPage?handle=hein.journals/amuilr36&div=28&id=&page= [Accessed 24 January 2022].

Thousand Year Dawn. (Marcel) by John Gerrard (2019) accessed on: 17/03/2021.
Available at: https://jbpichelski.co.uk/2019/01/29/thousand-year-dawn-marcel-by-john-gerrard/

True Artificial Intelligence will change everything. | Juergen Schmidhuber | TEDxLakeComo (no date) www.youtube.com. Available at: True Artificial Intelligence will change everything Juergen Schmidhuber | TEDxLakeComo [Accessed: 22 March 2021].

Wakefield, J., 2022. Elon Musk's Neuralink 'shows monkey playing Pong with mind'. [online] BBC News. Available at: https://www.bbc.co.uk/news/technology-56688812 [Accessed 24 January 2022].

Wilde, P. (202). I, Posthuman : embodying entangled subjectivities in gaming. [online] Ethos.bl.uk. Available at: https://ethos.bl.uk/OrderDetails.do?uin=uk.bl.ethos.732346 [Accessed 15 October 2021].

Wilson-Hughes, O. (2021). 'Maybe I'm tired of being human, if human is what I am' :sentimental posthumanism in the work of Martin Amis. [online] Ethos.bl.uk. Available at: https://ethos.bl.uk/OrderDetails.do?uin=uk.bl.ethos.657601. [Accessed 18 October 2021].

Wolfe, C., 2022. posthumanism. [online] Oxford Reference. Available at: https://www.oxfordreference.com/view/10.1093/oi/authority.20110803100339501 [Accessed 24 January 2022].

A note about Boom Graduates

We propel graduates forward so they can make their mark on the world - we push the boundaries, share brilliant ideas and inspire possibility. We publish dissertations as books, presented gift-boxed at graduation ceremonies, delivering brand-new research to the world quicker than anyone else. We plant trees for every commissioned book sold, and give our Boom graduates the chance to profit-share from their brilliant ideas. Furthermore we donate the majority of our profits to funding research and scholarship for disadvantaged students who wouldn't normally be able to attend university. Through academic excellence and environmental sustainability, *Boom Graduates* are changing the world.

We are Boom Graduates - an imprint of Boom Publications Ltd. We are a more-than-profit company, dedicating over half our profits to providing university scholarships for underprivileged students across the world. We aim to become the globe's biggest provider of such scholarships – and if like Euan, the author of this book, you'd also like to contribute to making the world a better place, please contact us: we publish monographs, edited books, and moreover our graduate series – Boom Graduates – are presented at graduation days across the world in archival, lined museum-quality presentation cases, engraved with the graduate's name and award.

Boom Publications are based at the Duncan of Jordanstone College of Art and Design, at the University of Dundee in Scotland. We were one of the winners of the 2022 Venture awards hosted by the Centre for Entrepreneurship, and have since been shortlisted for the Converge Challenge, a national award that brings together ambitious and creative thinkers with innovative ideas to work with industry experts to transform their ideas into sustainable companies operating in the commercial world. We are also climate conscious and work with agencies to plant a tree for each and every book commissioned, offsetting thousands of tonnes of carbon each year. Follow us on social media to watch our forest grow @boomgraduates.

Thank you for contributing by purchasing this book. Please visit our catalogues on www.boompublications.com.

Euan Rutter

An artist's perspective of posthumanism and AI

BOOM!

This book was originally submitted as a dissertation in partial fulfilment of the requirements of a Bachelor of Arts (Hons) degree in Fine Art at the Duncan of Jordanstone College of Art and Design, the University of Dundee, in 2022.

Euan Rutter

An artist's perspective of posthumanism and AI

Notes

Euan Rutter

An artist's perspective of posthumanism and AI

Euan Rutter

An artist's perspective of posthumanism and AI

Euan Rutter

//
An artist's perspective of posthumanism and AI

Euan Rutter

An artist's perspective of posthumanism and AI

Euan Rutter